After You Say "I Do"

H. NORMAN WRIGHT

HARVEST HOUSE PUBLISHERS
Eugene, Oregon 97402

Cover by Terry Dugan Design, Minneapolis, Minnesota

AFTER YOU SAY "I DO" (Revised and Expanded)

Copyright © 1999 by H. Norman Wright
Published by Harvest House Publishers
Eugene, Oregon 97402

ISBN 1-56507-991-4

Contents

ONE

What Is Marriage?

Marriage is one of the most important facets of your life. It contains unique and interesting potential. This guide has been developed to help you evaluate your marriage. I trust that as you work through this program, your present relationship will be strengthened to better ensure an enriching, fulfilling, and growing marriage. I also hope you will have a much more realistic perception of yourself, your spouse, and your marriage.

First of all, let's relive part of your courtship.

1. When did you meet? Describe this as well as you can remember. (By the way, can you remember what each of you was wearing?)

2. Who first wanted to date?

3. What did you like about the other person right at first?

4. When did you decide on the inside "you're for me"?

5. Who was the first person you told that you were engaged?

6. In what way is your spouse different than and similar to your parents?

7. Define marriage. What is its purpose?

8. How does your marriage relationship agree or differ from this definition and purpose?

9. Do you believe marriage is a contract?

10. How do you think your spouse would answer these questions?

Many people are propelled toward marriage without really understanding all they are committing themselves to for the rest of their lives. That is why couples experience surprises and upsets through the duration of their marriage. Marriage is many things:

- Marriage is a gift.

- Marriage is an opportunity for love to be learned.

- Marriage is a journey in which we, as the travelers, are faced with many choices—and we are responsible for those choices.

- Marriage is affected more by our inner communication than by our outer communication.

- Marriage is more often influenced by unresolved issues from our past than we realize.

- Marriage is a call to servanthood.

- Marriage is a call to friendship.

- Marriage is a call to suffering.

- Marriage is a refining process. It is an opportunity to be refined by God into the person He wants us to be.

- Marriage is not an event but a way of life.

- Marriage involves intimacy in all areas for it to be fulfilling. This intimacy must reach into the spiritual, the intellectual, the social, the emotional, and the physical.

- A marriage relationship is a school, a learning and growing environment in which (if everything is as it should be) both partners can grow and develop. The relationship grows along with them. If you can see marriage as an opportunity for growth, you can be satisfied and can satisfy your spouse.

Here is my own definition of marriage. Consider it carefully, and then talk over your feelings with your partner:

A Christian marriage is a total commitment of two people to the person of Jesus Christ and to each other. It is a commitment in which there is no holding back of anything. Marriage is a pledge of mutual fidelity; it is a partnership of mutual subordination. A Christian marriage is similar to a solvent; it is a freeing up of the man and woman to be themselves and become all that God intends for them to become. Marriage is a refining process that God will use to have us become the man or woman He wants us to become.

Think about it. God will use your marriage for His purpose. He will mold you for your own benefit and for His glory.

You may be thinking that in your marriage there are only two individuals involved. That is true, but there *is* a third party who can give even greater meaning to your individual and married life—that person is Jesus Christ. In what ways will you allow the presence of Jesus Christ in your life to make a difference in your marriage?

Read Genesis 2:18-25

1. Who originated the marriage institution?

2. What are the purposes of marriage, and why was it originated? (See Genesis 1:28; 2:18; Ephesians 5:22-32.)

   a.

   b.

   c.

   d.

3. How is marriage good? (See Genesis 2:18; Hebrews 13:4.)

4. In your opinion, what is a helpmeet? In your spouse's opinion?

5. What does leaving mother and father involve?

6. What do the words *shall cleave* mean?

7. What do the words *they shall be one flesh* mean to you?

8. List six behaviors that you presently perform in marriage to promote and maintain the oneness characteristic of marriage.

   a.

   b.

   c.

   d.

   e.

   f.

   Leave and *cleave*—different words, significant words. When you exchanged your wedding vows, these two words became

part of your life. But do you understand them? To leave means to sever one relationship before establishing another. This does not mean you disregard your parents. Rather it requires that you break your tie to them and assume responsibility for your spouse.

To cleave means to weld together. When a man cleaves to his wife they become one flesh. This term is a beautiful capsule description of the oneness, completeness, and permanence God intended in the marriage relationship. It suggests a unique oneness—a total commitment to intimacy in all of life together, symbolized by the sexual union.

Years ago I heard a choice description of the coming together that is involved in cleaving. If you hold a lump of dark green clay in one hand and a lump of light green clay in the other hand, you can clearly identify the two different shades of color. However, when you mold the two lumps together, you see just one lump of green clay—at first glance. When you inspect the lump closely you see the distinct and separate lines of dark and light green clay.

This is a picture of your marriage relationship. The two of you are blended together so you appear as one, yet you each retain your own distinct identity and personality. But now you also have a marriage personality that exists in the two of you.

A Christian marriage, however, involves more than the blending of two people. It also includes a third person, Jesus Christ, who gives meaning, guidance, and direction to the relationship. When He presides in a marriage, then and only then is it a Christian marriage.

Since your wedding, how have you handled leaving your parents? How have you become one flesh, coming together and yet retaining who you are as individuals? Why not talk about it?

1. List three of the most important Scripture verses upon which you would like to base your continuing marriage relationship. (Please use passages other than Ephesians 5:21-33, 1 Corinthians 13, and 1 Peter 3 because most couples automatically look to these. They are important, but think through other important passages that will assist you in establishing the type of marriage you are seeking.)

   a.

   b.

   c.

Read Matthew 7:24-27

This passage is talking about building your house upon a firm foundation. List what you believe are ten firm foundations you will use to make a solid marriage relationship.

   1.

   2.

   3.

   4.

   5.

   6.

   7.

   8.

   9.

   10.

Reasons for Marriage

There are many reasons and motivating factors for marriage. What are yours? Have you ever thought about them? Here are two very important questions for you to answer and then discuss with your spouse.

1. What are you receiving out of marriage that you wouldn't have received by remaining single?

2. On a separate piece of paper, list the reasons why you married your spouse. After you have done that, list the reasons why you think your spouse married you. Then share the results.

Evaluate your "marriageability" by examining the personality traits of yourself and your spouse. List eight character or personality traits you feel have helped your marriage.

   1.

   2.

   3.

   4.

5.

6.

7.

8.

In your Bible turn to Galatians 5:22,23, and read over the fruit of the Spirit. Would these traits manifested in a person give him or her a greater potential of success in marriage? If so, indicate which of these you manifest and which of them you are still having difficulty displaying.

In addition to utilizing the fruit of the Spirit as a guide for evaluating a marriage, eight marriageability traits have been isolated that give a person a greater possibility of having an enriched and satisfying marriage.

1. Adaptability and flexibility—the ability to change and adapt

2. Empathy—the ability to be sensitive to the needs, hurts, and desires of others, to feel with them and experience the world from their perspective

3. Ability to work through problems

4. Ability to give and receive love

5. Emotional stability—accepting one's emotions and controlling them

6. Communication

7. Similarities between the couple themselves

8. Similar family background

The natural inclination is to look at this list and say, "Oh yes, that's us. We are like that and have these characteristics." If you feel these traits are present, give a specific example of how each of the first six traits was manifested in the past two weeks. Then, for traits 7 and 8, give examples of the similarity for each one.

1.

2.

3.

4.

5.

6.

7.

8.

Two

Evaluating Your Marriage

*L*et's look at your marriage. This is your opportunity to evaluate where you are at the present time.

1. Describe how much significant time you spend together as a couple and when you spend it.

2. Describe five behaviors or tasks that your partner does that you appreciate.

3. List five personal qualities of your spouse you appreciate.

4. How frequently do you affirm or reinforce your spouse for the behaviors and qualities described in questions 2 and 3?

5. List four important requests you have for your spouse at this time.

How frequently do you make these requests?

What is your spouse's response?

6. List four important requests your spouse has for you at this time.

How frequently does he/she make these requests?

What is your response?

7. What do you appreciate most about your partner's communication?

8. What could be improved in your partner's communication?

9. List five expectations you have for your spouse.

Indicate with a check mark which ones are being met at this time.

10. List five expectations your spouse has for you.

Indicate with a check mark which ones are being met at this time.

11. What do you do to let your spouse know you love him/her?

12. What does your spouse do to let you know he/she loves you?

13. Level of Marital Satisfaction: Draw a line that indicates your level of satisfaction over the length of your marriage. If you need to change the numbers at the bottom of the graph, please feel free to do so. Then use a dotted or broken line to indicate what you believe to be your spouse's level of marital satisfaction over the length of your marriage.

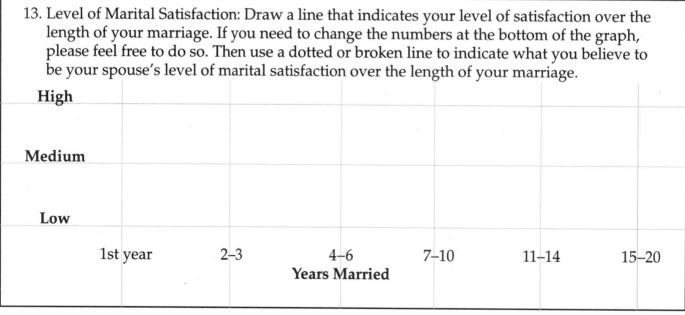

High

Medium

Low

1st year   2–3   4–6   7–10   11–14   15–20

Years Married

14. What has been one of the most fulfilling experiences in your marriage?

What has been one of the most upsetting experiences in your marriage?

15. What personal and marital behaviors would you like to change in yourself?

What personal and marital behaviors would you like to see changed in your partner?

What personal and marital behaviors would your spouse like to see changed in you?

Current Level of Satisfaction

Use an X to indicate your level of satisfaction. (Zero means no satisfaction, 5 is average and 10 means super, fantastic, the best.) Use a circle to indicate what you think your partner's level of satisfaction is at the present time.

1. Our daily personal involvement with each other

0 1 2 3 4 5 6 7 8 9 10

2. Our affectionate romantic interaction

0 1 2 3 4 5 6 7 8 9 10

3. Our sexual relationship

0 1 2 3 4 5 6 7 8 9 10

4. The frequency of our sexual contact

0 1 2 3 4 5 6 7 8 9 10

5. My trust in my spouse

0 1 2 3 4 5 6 7 8 9 10

6. My spouse's trust in me

0 1 2 3 4 5 6 7 8 9 10

7. The depth of our communication together

0 1 2 3 4 5 6 7 8 9 10

8. How well we speak one another's language

_____

0 1 2 3 4 5 6 7 8 9 10

9. The way we divide chores

_____

0 1 2 3 4 5 6 7 8 9 10

10. The way we make decisions

_____

0 1 2 3 4 5 6 7 8 9 10

11. The way we manage conflict

_____

0 1 2 3 4 5 6 7 8 9 10

12. Adjustments to one another's differences

_____

0 1 2 3 4 5 6 7 8 9 10

13. Amount of free time together

_____

0 1 2 3 4 5 6 7 8 9 10

14. Quality of free time together

_____

0 1 2 3 4 5 6 7 8 9 10

15. Amount of free time apart

_____

0 1 2 3 4 5 6 7 8 9 10

16. Our interaction with friends as a couple

_____

0 1 2 3 4 5 6 7 8 9 10

17. The way we support each other in rough times

_____

0 1 2 3 4 5 6 7 8 9 10

18. The way we support each other's careers

_____

0 1 2 3 4 5 6 7 8 9 10

19. Our spiritual interaction

_____

0 1 2 3 4 5 6 7 8 9 10

20. Our church involvement

_____

0 1 2 3 4 5 6 7 8 9 10

21. The level of our financial security

_____

0 1 2 3 4 5 6 7 8 9 10

22. How we manage money

_____

0 1 2 3 4 5 6 7 8 9 10

23. My spouse's relationship with my relatives

_____

0 1 2 3 4 5 6 7 8 9 10

24. My relationship with my spouse's relatives

_____

0 1 2 3 4 5 6 7 8 9 10

Select any three that have a score of 3 or less and indicate what needs to occur for you to have a higher level of satisfaction. Also list what you have already tried to do.

THREE

Uniqueness and Acceptance in Marriage

Your partner is not you. He or she is "other," created in God's image, not yours. He or she has a right to be other, to be treated and respected as other.

Before you married you probably had a preconceived fantasy of your ideal mate or the perfect marriage. After a while you began to realize that your fantasy and the person you have married diverge sharply. At that point you may have embarked upon a reform program, forgetting that only God can make a person. You misconstrued the words of the wedding ceremony and "the two shall become one" to mean that your mate should become like you and your fantasy. You thought you would become one in likes, preferences, interests, hobbies, ideas, even reactions and feelings—yours! The oneness in marriage is not similarity or sameness in matters relating to ideas or feelings, but it's the oneness of *understanding.* Any attempt to mold our mates in an effort to match them to our fantasies is arrogance on our part and an insult to them. While it is true that we can never mold or remake another person, we can "allow" them to change.

The instruction on right living in Ephesians 4:2 can be applied to the marriage relationship: "[…Living as becomes you] with complete lowliness of mind (humility) and meekness (unselfishness, gentleness, mildness), with patience, bearing with one another and making allowances because you love one another" (AMP). Look again at the last part of the verse: "making allowances because you love one another." List six specific examples of how this portion could be applied in your marriage relationship. Try to think of these in relation to your differentness.

1.

2.

3.

4.

5.

6.

Fill in the answers to the next section.

Similarities	Differences	Effect
How are my spouse and I similar?	How are my spouse and I different?	How can these differences or similarities complement or help us in our marriage?

Which of the differences have you thanked God for?

Differences —The Potential for Growth and Enhancement

Every person who marries has characteristics similar to the one he or she marries. But there are also many differences. Different ways of perceiving, thinking, feeling, and behaving are part of marital adjustment. Differentness is important because it holds out the promise of need fulfillment for each person. It is vital to remember that one of the main motivating factors toward marriage is the person's need to feel complete because of what the other person has to offer. Consciously or unconsciously, people choose others who can help them feel complete.

Our innate differentness also contains the seeds for hurt and disruption. Why? The answer is quite simple: We are threatened by the differences in our spouses. We are afraid that we might have to adjust our way of thinking and doing things. We also tend to believe that "if it's different, it's wrong." Many problems occur because of the lack of tolerance for differences of attitude or opinions in the marital relationship. Problems occur because we did not allow the other person to be different. But consider these thoughts:

In the midst of the marital struggle the honeymoon dream vanishes, and the despair over the old relationship comes up for reexamination. Suddenly each spouse turns his eyes away from the partner and looks inwardly and asks, "What am I doing to my partner? What is wrong with me? What am I misunderstanding? What must I do to rescue this marriage?" If honestly asked, the answers are not far behind: "I really married my wife because of her difference. It is not my job to make her over, but rather to discover and to value that difference. But before I can do that I must accept my difference, and I really need her to help me discover my uniqueness. My task is not to mold her into a beautiful vase, but to participate with her to discover that beautiful vase even as we discover it in me. How arrogant of me to think I could shape another human being! How humble it makes me to realize that I need to yield to another and thereby be changed! Our relationship will change both of us—in a process of being shaped into a form far more beautiful than either could imagine."

We try to change people to conform to our ideas of how they should be. So does God. But there the similarity ends. Our ideas of what the other person should do or how he should act may be an improvement or an imprisonment. We may be setting the other person free of behavior patterns that are restricting his development, or we may be simply chaining him up in another behavioral bondage.[1]

1. If you are definitely bothered by the uniqueness of your spouse, ask yourself, "What would it be like being married to a person just like me—and would I like it?"

2. In what way will the presence of Jesus Christ in your life help you adjust to differences in your marriage?

FOUR

Love as a Basis for Marriage

***M**ost couples say they are married because they love their spouses. Let's assume for a minute that in order to be married you had to convince a jury in a court of law that you really did love the other person. Write in detail the facts you would present to a jury. Include in your presentation your definition of love.*

What does it mean to love another person in terms of daily living? Here are a number of responses given by individuals who were asked to define a loving relationship:

A loving relationship is a choice partnership. Loving someone in which even imperfection is seen as possibility and, therefore, a thing of beauty; where discovery,

struggle and acceptance are the basis of continued growth and wonderment.

A loving relationship is one in which individuals trust each other enough to become vulnerable, secure that the other person won't take advantage. It neither exploits nor takes the other for granted. It involves much communication, much sharing, and much tenderness.

A loving relationship is one in which one can be open and honest with another without the fear of being judged. It's being secure in the knowledge that you are each other's best friend and no matter what happens you will stand by one another.

A loving relationship is one which offers comfort in the silent presence of another with whom you know, through words or body language, you share mutual trust, honesty, admiration, devotion, and that special thrill of happiness simply being together.

A loving relationship is an undemanding exchange of affection and concern, rooted in total honesty and continuing communication without exploitation.

A loving relationship is one in which the loved one is free to be himself—to laugh with me, but never at me; to cry with me, but never because of me; to love life, to love himself, to love being loved. Such a relationship is based upon freedom and can never grow in a jealous heart.

A loving relationship is one in which each one sees the beloved not as an extension of self but as a unique, forever become, beautiful individual—a situation in which the persons can bring their own special "I" to each other, a blending of selves without the fear of loss of self.[1]

In light of the various ideas and definitions of love given so far, complete the following sentences:

1. The way I would like to give love to my spouse is…

2. The way I would like to receive love from my spouse is…

3. The specific ways I could show my love even more are…

4. The specific ways my spouse could show his/her love more are…

5. What I really appreciate about the way my spouse loves me is…

No matter how deep your love for your spouse may be, it will be unknown to him/her unless it is openly and consistently expressed in a manner that registers with your partner. Far too many marriage partners are silent and passive in their expressions of love. God has called us to be vessels of love pouring generously to our partners. Marriage is God's creative gift to us, providing us the opportunity to express love to its fullest in the safety and security of an abiding relationship. And we are only able to love because God first loved us. His love is so extensive that it can heal the loveless experiences of the past. We no longer need to be dominated by hurtful memories. Instead we can live and love knowing the adequacy of Jesus Christ in our lives.[2]

What does the Word of God say about love? Look up the following passages of Scripture to discover love from God's perspective. (I suggest using a modern translation.) What is the central thought or example in each passage?

Reference	*The Biblical Concept of Love*
1. Proverbs 17:17	
2. Matthew 6:24	
3. Matthew 22:37-39	
4. Luke 6:27-35	
5. Luke 10:25-37	
6. John 3:16	
7. John 13:34	
8. Romans 13:8-10	
9. Romans 14:15	
10. 1 Corinthians 8:1	
11. Galatians 2:20	
12. Galatians 5:13	
13. Galatians 6:2	
14. Ephesians 4:2	
15. Ephesians 5:2	
16. Ephesians 5:25	
17. Titus 2:3-5	
18. 1 Peter 4:8	
19. 1 John 3:16-18	

Three Types of Love:
Eros, Philia, Agape

Eros is the love that seeks sensual expression. It is a romantic love, a sexual love inspired by the biological structure of human nature. A husband and wife, in a good marriage, will love each other romantically and erotically.

In a good marriage the husband and wife are also friends. Friendship means companionship, communication, and cooperation. This is known as *philia*.

Agape is self-giving love, gift love, the love that goes on loving even when the other becomes unlovable. *Agape love is not something that just happens to you; it's something you make happen.* Love is a personal act of commitment. Christ's love (the pattern for our love) is gift love. His love for us is a sacrificial love. His love is unconditional. Christ's love is an eternal love. Agape is kindness. It is being sympathetic, thoughtful, and sensitive to the needs of your loved one. Agape is contentment. Agape is forgiving love.

If individuals would put forth effort to increase philia and agape love, all three types of love would increase. The friendship love of philia can enhance and enrich both of the others. Both agape and philia can enrich the eros love so it doesn't diminish as much as it usually does. It, too, can flourish if properly nurtured, and if so, the other types of love are reinforced. But *all three* must be given conscious effort.

In your marriage what can you do to demonstrate these three types of love? Under each word write five specific examples of what you will do to enhance your love relationship.

Eros	Philia	Agape
1.	1.	1.
2.	2.	2.
3.	3.	3.
4.	4.	4.
5.	5.	5.

What do you feel are the three main hindrances in a couple's marriage to developing love and continuing to grow?

1.

2.

3.

Your love will either live or die. What kills love? Love dies when you spend little or no time together and when you stop sharing activities that are mutually enjoyable. Love is created or destroyed by pairing or failing to pair the partner with pleasurable activities over a period of time. Attempting to control the other, as well as excessive anger, will also kill love. Love dies from failure on the part of both individuals to reinforce appropriate behavior in each other. Smiling, caressing, complimenting, showing compassion, and spending time together are behaviors in marriage that may not be reinforced. If they are not, they may disappear. If your partner stops doing things that you like, your love feelings may disappear.

1. What do you do now to reinforce the behaviors from your spouse that you enjoy?

2. Without asking your spouse, what behaviors does he/she enjoy from you? (The "Cherishing Days" list beginning on page 27 will really help you.)

Many couples feel they have tried to demonstrate love and meet the needs of their spouses but keep missing the mark. To eliminate misunderstanding and mind reading, it is far better to share with one another your needs, wants, and desires in a specific yet nondemanding manner. When you seek to learn your partner's wishes in order to meet them as best you can, you are implementing the model of servanthood as portrayed in the Scripture.

One of the most effective ways of meeting each other's love needs and wants is to launch into the "Cherishing Days" exercise. Sound interesting? It can be very interesting, and it is easy to implement. Each partner makes a list of small cherishing behaviors that he or she would enjoy receiving from the other. These requested behaviors should have four characteristics:

a. They must be specific and positive. For example, a wife would like her husband to sit next to her on the couch as they watch the news after dinner. She has made a positive request for a desired behavior instead of complaining, "You ignore me and are preoccupied with the TV."

b. The small cherishing behaviors must not be concerned with past conflicts or old demands.

c. The positive behaviors must be such that they can be accomplished on an everyday basis.

d. The behaviors must be achievable—they do not require excessive time or expense.

Take several days to compile your lists. Think back to the most satisfying times of your courtship and marriage to discover ideas for your list. Some of the behaviors you think of may seem trivial or somewhat embarrassing to you. It's perfectly all right. Include them on your list as long as they reflect valid personal wants or needs.

Once your list of 15 to 20 cherishing behaviors is completed, exchange lists with your partner and discuss the cherishing behaviors you are requesting from each other. Be sure to tell your spouse *how* you would like each behavior performed for you. For example, if you request a back rub at bedtime, specify light skin rub or deep muscle massage, with lotion or without, and so on. As you discuss your written requests, feel free to add others to the list as you think of them.

After your discussion, declare the next seven days to be "Cherishing Days." Make a commitment to put your partner's list into practice. Try to accomplish as many of the cherishing behaviors on the list as possible each day. Focus your attention and energies on what you do for your spouse, not what he/she does for you. At the end of seven days you may evaluate whether you will continue the exercise for another week.

Why does this encourage love and romance so well? Because the list of positive behaviors that you exchange consists of requested, discussed, and agreed upon acts of love. The guesswork of "What shall I do for him/her? Will he/she like it?" is eliminated. Also, the commitment is short term—you are only responsible for seven days. And the behaviors are purposely simple and easily achievable. The margin of failure is greatly reduced.

Another important factor in the success of this exercise is the commitment of each individual to the "I must change first" principle. You are not keeping score of your spouse's efforts. You are too busy concentrating on accomplishing his/her list. And with each behavior comes a positive response, which encourages the giver to continue. As each person gives and receives positive loving acts, the bond of love will grow stronger.

Most couples decide to continue the exercise after completing the seven-day commitment. They find that the positives of filling each others' wants and needs eliminate the negatives of love-recessive behavior patterns. The "Cherishing Days" exercise is a practical, simple application of scriptural admonitions to kindness, love, edification, and more.

Here is a sample list of cherishing behaviors that many people have found helpful.

Cherishing Days

- Greet me with a hug and kiss before we get out of bed in the morning.

- When you're out walking, bring back a flower or a leaf.

- Look at me and smile.

- Call me during the day and tell me something pleasant.

- Turn off the lights and light a candle when we have dinner.

- Put on a favorite record and come sit next to me and hold my hand.

- Ask me how I spent my day.

- Wash my back in the tub or shower.

- Pick me up at work or at the bus stop as a surprise.

- Put a surprise note in my lunch or article of clothing.

- Tell me how much you enjoy having breakfast with me.

- Tell the children (in front of me) that I'm a good parent.

- When we sit together, put your arm around me.

- Have coffee with me in the morning before we wake the children so we can have a five-minute talk together.

- Take me on a date and make all the arrangements.

- Hold me at night before we go to sleep.

- Ask my opinion about world affairs or the sermon at church.

- For no special reason hug me and say you love me.

- Greet me with a smile when we first see each other at the end of the day.

- Use endearing words with me sometime.

- When we are out, wink or blow a kiss to me.[3]

This list is just a sample. I'm sure you can add ideas of your own to the list.

3. How will the presence of Jesus Christ in your life help you to love your spouse through eros, philia, and agape love?

FIVE

What Did You Expect?

Every person who marries enters the marriage relationship with certain expectations. These expectations come from many sources, including parents, society, books, public speakers, and our own ideas. It is very important to take the time to find out what these expectations were and are, which are realistic, which can be achieved in your marriage, and how to handle them when things do not go according to plan. The word expectation carries with it the attitude of hope. Hope has been defined as "the anticipation of something good." Hope is necessary because it motivates us and often keeps us going.

The next exercise will take some thought and time on your part. Think about the expectations you have of your spouse. These can be simple or elaborate. For example, a husband might expect his wife to:

- be at the door when he arrives home
- always be at home and never work
- have sex with him whenever he wants it.

A wife might expect her husband to:

- go to her parents' house with her whenever she goes
- be the spiritual leader in their home
- spend Saturdays at home and not out hunting

List your expectations now, but do not discuss them with your partner yet. You will be using the columns on the right later.

	C	S	N
1. _____			
2. _____			
3. _____			
4. _____			
5. _____			
6. _____			
7. _____			
8. _____			
9. _____			
10. _____			
11. _____			
12. _____			
13. _____			
14. _____			
15. _____			
16. _____			
17. _____			
18. _____			
19. _____			
20. _____			

Now list ten expectations you think your partner has for you in marriage.

1.

2.

3.

4.

5.

6.

7.

8.

9.

10.

Let's briefly talk about disappointment. We all experience disappointments because some of our expectations, hopes, and dreams are not realized. List three of the most disappointing experiences of your life, and then indicate what you did or how you handled the disappointment.

1.

2.

3.

Now let's go back to your 20 expectations for your spouse. Take each expectation and, on a separate piece of paper, write one or two sentences indicating how your marriage relationship is affected if this expectation isn't met.

Now take this list of expectations and share it with your partner. Take your partner's list and read it to yourself. As you read each one of your partner's expectations of you, place a check mark in the appropriate column: **C** stands for "cinch"; you feel that the expectation is a cinch to fulfill. **S** stands for "sweat"; it takes some hard work and sweat but it can be done. **N** stands for "no way"; you feel that the expectation is impossible. When the two of you have completed your evaluation of the expectations give them back and spend some time discussing them.

There are three very common expectations that couples have for their marriage. Couples expect their marriage to work out and never end in divorce. This is an excellent goal, but what are you doing to make it a reality? Write a paragraph indicating what you personally are doing to make your marriage work. When you and your spouse have done this, share your paragraphs together.

Couples also expect their marriage to progress smoothly onward and upward without any major upheavals or adjustments. Consider the following suggested outline of the three stages of marriage.

Three Stages of Marriage
(and some words and ideas that go with these stages)[1]

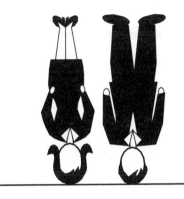

Enchantment	*Disenchantment*	*Maturity*
On Cloud 9	Upset	Feet on the ground
Perfect	Terrible	I need you
Just right	Absolutely wrong	How do you see it?
Forever	I quit	Let's work it out
Infatuated	Hurt	I'll help you
Idolize	Put down	Encourage
Numb	Splintered	Whole
Fascinated	Irritated	Refreshed
Charmed	Wretched	Thankful
Captivated	Burdened	Free
Ecstasy	Uncomfortable	Comfortable
Thrilled	Bitter	Friendly
Preoccupied	Trapped	Growing
We've arrived	We'll never make it	Together we can make it

It has been suggested that all couples go through these three stages. What about you? Perhaps in your own relationship you have experienced some of the words in the various stages already. Circle any of the words in the three stages that indicate how you have felt at one time or another in your marriage. Then underline the words that describe your current state. When you have finished writing, share your responses together.

Often many of our expectations come from our own homes and our backgrounds. Complete the following statements and then share your responses with your partner.

1. This is what you need to know about my family life as I was growing up in order to understand me:

2. If I could have changed one thing about my family life as I was growing up, it would have been . . .

3. Because I want or don't want this to occur in my own marriage and family life I am . . .

4. My parents have influenced my attitudes about marriage by . . .

5. Something from my parents' marriage that I want to have in mine is . . .

6. Something from my parents' marriage that I prefer not to have in mine is . . .

7. Talk with your partner and list, on a separate piece of paper, ten similarities and ten differences about his/her home and family life and yours. Discuss these together. How are any of these affecting your own marriage?

Marriage is always full of twists and turns, bends in the road, U-turns, even temporary roadblocks and seeming dead ends. The journey uniquely blends acquiring and losing, receiving and giving away, holding and letting go. A loving, committed relationship helps us weather all of these moves.

From birth until death, life is a series of transitions, a series of bridges between different stages of life. A transition is a period of moving from one period of certainty to a new period of certainty. But in-between there is a period of uncertainty. What can we do when we're in the midst of a transitional struggle? First we need to identify what is making the adjustment particularly difficult. This can affect the health of our marriages. The problem may be a normal change of life or an unexpected event, but most problems encountered during such a transition center on one of the following:

1. Difficulty separating from the past stage; uncomfortable with our new roles

2. Difficulty making decisions concerning what new path to take and what plan of action to follow

3. Difficulty carrying out this new decision due to lack of understanding of what is involved in making the change, lacking of information concerning expectations for ourselves and others, or lack of preparation

4. Difficulty weathering the period of adjustment until the new changes have stabilized, due to possible lack of information or resources needed to make the change secure

Some transitions are quite normal, but nonetheless involve major changes. People marry, have children, the children go to school and then move into adolescence and adulthood. Other events can be more wrenching, affecting us in ways we never expected. Positive events such as a move, a promotion, the birth of twins, or finally having a baby after 17 years of being without can have the same effect. A sudden change can become a threat to whatever marital balance has been achieved.

During any major transition, people must restructure how they view their roles in life and plan how to incorporate changes. Write how you would react to the following circumstances that could cause changes in your marriage:

1. a miscarriage

2. death of a child

3. major financial difficulty

4. being fired from a job

5. wife working instead of the husband

6. major personal illness

7. being involved in a major lawsuit of potentially great financial loss and severe emotional stress

8. living in an apartment instead of the home you were in for five years

9. living in the country instead of the city

10. husband quitting his job to go into business for himself

11. wife wanting to go to work while leaving three children at home

12. child does not turn out the way you wanted

13. two more children than you planned on having

14. children leaving home

15. your parents becoming dependent upon you

If you find that you are facing or are in the midst of a transition, here are some suggestions:

1. Look at the stage of life you are leaving. Are you fighting leaving it in any way? What do you not want to give up or change? What makes you uncomfortable with this new role? What would make you more comfortable? Find someone with whom you can discuss your responses to these questions.

2. If you are having difficulty making a decision regarding a new change or determining what plan to follow, seek the advice of someone you respect whose insights will help you.

3. Make a specific list of what is involved in making this change. Look for the information through reading and asking others about their own experiences.

4. Spend time reading the book of Psalms. Many of the psalms reflect the struggles of humanity, but they also give the comfort and assurance that are from God's mercies.

5. Identify specifically what you need to do at this time that will help you feel as

though you have some control of the situation. And remember, being in control does not mean you have all of the answers or you know the outcome or when the situation will be resolved. Being in control means you have given yourself permission not to have all of these questions answered. You have told yourself that you can handle the uncertainty. Being in control means you have allowed Jesus Christ to come and stand with you in this time of uncertainty. His presence gives you the stability and control you need.

Christ's strength is what you need. "My grace is sufficient for thee: for my strength is made perfect in weakness" (2 Corinthians 12:9 KJV). Look back at James 1:2,3. The word *count* or *consider* means "an internal attitude of heart and mind that causes the trial and circumstance of life to affect a person either adversely or beneficially." The verse tense used here means this is a decisive giving up or resignation. Another interpretation of this could be "to make up your mind to regard adversities as something to welcome or be glad about." It is an attitude of the mind.

The word *trials* means "outward trouble or stress, or disappointments, sorrow, or hardships." These are situations that you had no part in bringing about. They are not sinful; they just happened. They are all of the various sorts of trouble that we have in our lives.

The word *endurance,* or *patience,* as it is sometimes translated, means "fortitude" or "the quality of being stabilized or remaining alive." It is, in a sense, a picture of standing firm under pressure rather than trying to escape.

How will the presence of Jesus Christ in your life help you fulfill your expectations of marriage and accept the ones that are not fulfilled?

SIX

Goals in Marriage

⟶⟵

Less than three percent of married couples have set goals for their marriage. Goals are vital; unless you have something in mind that you want to work toward or achieve, you will not get very far. What goals do you have for your marriage? What do you want your marriage to become? What do you want it to reflect?

You might also think in terms of the various aspects of your relationship: intellectual, physical, emotional, spiritual, social, financial. What goals would you like to achieve in each of these areas?

We all want to be happy in our marriage relationship, but that is too broad a goal. Goals need to be more specific. For a goal to be a good one, it must have three characteristics: 1) It must be specific (well-defined, to the point); 2) It must be realistic and/or attainable; 3) It must have a time limit (next week, this summer, in 20 years—someday does not count).

List six goals for your marriage on the goal wheel below. Write one goal in each of six spaces. Then take one of the remaining spaces and write a goal that you personally would like to achieve within three to five years. In the remaining space write a goal that you would like to see your spouse achieve within three to five years. Remember, a goal should be specific, realistic, attainable, and have a time limit.

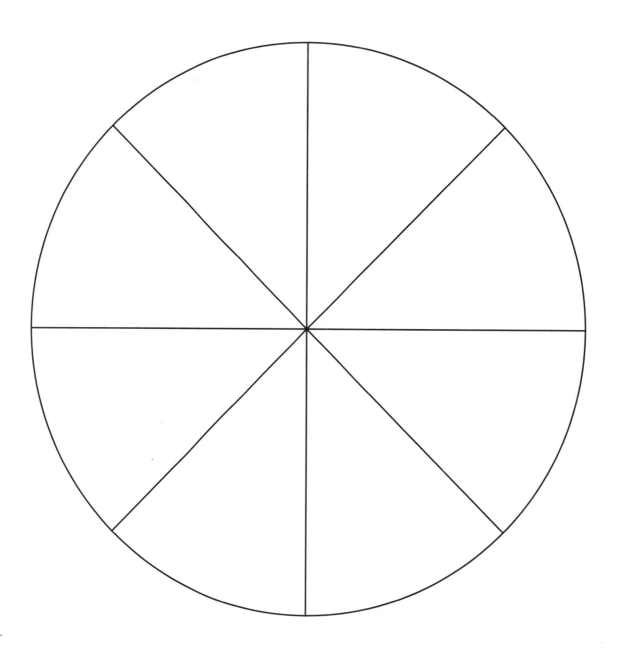

Now follow these directions concerning your goals.

1. Place an * by four of the eight goals that you feel are the most important. Then rank them in order of importance.

2. Place a **0** by any two of the eight goals that you would be willing to forego if absolutely necessary.

3. Place a **$** by the ones that cost money.

4. Place a **P** by the ones you learned from your parents.

5. Place an **S** by the ones you think your spouse wrote down.

6. Give a one-sentence explanation of why your marriage goals are important to the health of your marriage.

7. Now share and discuss your goals with your spouse.

8. Having goals is great—scary, but great! But now the good works begins. Look at your goals as statements of faith in God. "We can make our plans, but the final outcome is in God's hands…. Commit your work to the Lord, then it will succeed" (Proverbs 16:1,3 TLB). "Live life then, with a due sense of responsibility, not as men and women who do not know the meaning and purpose of life, but as those who do" (Ephesians 5:15,16 PHILLIPS). A goal is a statement about how we hope things are going to be in the future.

Now, select two of your marriage goals that are the most similar and develop a plan to reach them. You will need to take some mini-steps to reach the longer goal you listed. Remember that these short-term goals still need those three characteristics that make a goal a good one. It is important to periodically evaluate and determine your goals because goals do change.

How will the presence of Jesus Christ in your life assist you in setting and achieving your goals?

SEVEN

Fulfilling Intimacy Needs

◇

One of the motivating factors for marriage is the fulfillment of needs in one's life. It is admirable to say that we are marrying the other person in order to help him or her fulfill his or her needs; but, to be very honest, we do hope and believe that our needs will be met too. In marriage counseling, one of the major complaints couples bring in is that of not having their needs met. Often one partner is attempting to meet the needs of the other, but the other partner doesn't always know what the needs are or he or she doesn't know exactly how to meet them.

It is important for married people to define their needs specifically and then indicate how they would like their partners to respond in order to meet those needs. Some have asked, "Doesn't it take the romance out of marriage if you have to tell the other person exactly what you need?" Not really. In fact, it can increase the romance because your spouse won't have to play the game of mind reading to figure out what you need and what you want!

Intimacy needs are the heart of a marriage. The word *intimacy* actually means "inmost." Intimacy suggests a very strong personal relationship, a special *emotional* closeness that includes understanding and being understood by someone who is very special. Intimacy has also been defined as "an affectionate bond, the strands of which are composed of mutual caring, responsibility, trust, open communication of feelings and sensations, as well as the non-defended interchange of information about significant events." Intimacy means taking the risk to be close to someone and allowing that someone to step inside your personal boundaries.

Sometimes intimacy can hurt. As you lower your defenses to let each other close, you reveal the real, intimate, secret you to each other, including your weaknesses and faults. With the real you exposed, you become vulnerable to possible ridicule from your partner. The potential for pain is there, but the rewards of intimacy greatly overshadow that risk. Intimacy means vulnerability, but it also means security. The openness can be scary, but the acceptance each partner offers in the midst of vulnerability provides a sense of security. Intimate couples can feel safe and accepted—fully exposed, perhaps, yet fully accepted.

Take a moment to evaluate the intimacy in your marriage relationship. Explore how you deal with intimacy as a couple by circling your response to the following statements. Work through the exercise separately, then explain your responses to each other:

1. When it comes to conversational intimacy, the way I see our relationship is . . .

   a. We say a lot but reveal little of our real selves.

   b. We reveal our real selves but we don't say very much.

   c. We say a lot and reveal a lot of our real selves.

   d. We say little and reveal little of our real selves.

2. When it comes to sharing with you what I am really thinking, feeling, wanting, or not wanting . . .

   a. I keep my inner self well hidden.

   b. I reveal as much as I feel safe sharing.

   c. I let it all hang out.

3. When it comes to sharing with me what you are really thinking, feeling, wanting, or not wanting . . .

   a. You seem to keep your inner self well hidden.

   b. You seem to reveal as much as you feel safe to share.

   c. You seem to let it all hang out.

4. Some ways I avoid intimacy when we are getting uncomfortably close are . . .

   a. I laugh or crack a joke.

   b. I shrug it off and act as if it doesn't matter.

   c. I act confused—like I don't know what is going on.

   d. I look angry so you can't see into me too deeply.

   e. I get angry or huffy, especially when I am feeling vulnerable.

   f. I get very talkative.

   g. I get analytical—hiding behind a wall of intellectualizing.

   h. I change the subject so I won't have to deal with it.

   i. I act strong, together, above-it-all— especially when I'm feeling vulnerable.

5. The reason I avoid intimacy this way is . . .

6. The effect of avoiding intimacy in this way is . . .

7. From the list on the previous page, some ways I see my spouse avoid intimacy when we are getting uncomfortably close are . . .

8. In order to build intimacy in our relationship, I would now be willing to . . .[1]

Now take your Bible and look for the passages that say God has promised to meet every need on your list. Instead of relying on ourselves or our spouses to meet our needs, we find that God has promises for us that will give us the stability we are seeking. You may want to start with the following references. To which area of your needs do these relate?

1. Psalm 103:4

2. Matthew 6:33,34

3. Romans 5:8; 8:35,39

4. Ephesians 2:10

Now evaluate the level of response on each of the six dimensions of intimacy. Indicate the level for your marriage by placing an X on the line. Share your responses together, and then discuss what you could do to improve the level in each dimension.

1. *Emotional Intimacy.* You feel close to one another. You feel emotionally supported and cared for by your mate. There is a sharing of hurts and joys and a sense that each of you is genuinely interested in the well-being of the other.

0————————5————————10

2. *Social Intimacy.* You have many friends in common as opposed to socializing sepa-

rately. Having time together with mutual friends is an important part of your shared activities.

0————————5————————10

3. *Sexual Intimacy.* True sexual intimacy involves more than the mere performance of the sex act. In truly intimate marriages, sexual expression is an essential part of the relationship. It is a communication vehicle and not just a duty. Genuine interest, satisfaction, ability to discuss sexual issues . . . these are characteristics of a sexually intimate relationship.

0————————5————————10

4. *Intellectual Intimacy.* Intellectual intimacy involves the sharing of ideas. In short, when you are intellectually intimate, you talk to each other. More than just superficial conversations about the weather, you seek input from your mate regarding issues of importance. You value your mate's opinion and want to share your own.

0————————5————————10

5. *Recreational Intimacy.* You enjoy and share in many of the same "just for fun" activities. You have many similar interests.

0————————5————————10

6. *Spiritual Intimacy.* For you to be spiritually intimate, three criteria must be met:
   a. You must share common or similar beliefs about God.

   b. These beliefs must be important and significant to your lives.

   c. You must honestly share where you are in your own spiritual quest.

0————————5————————10

Intimacy involves the sharing of emotions. Consider this definition of emotions:

Our emotions are the movements of our soul. They are the sensations we experience that bear the labels of joy, grief, pain, disillusionment, love, delight, warmth, astonishment, fright. They are the stirring of our inner persons reflected in our cellular shells. Also, emotions are the subterranean shifts in feeling we encounter that aren't necessarily activated by sight, hearing, taste, or smell—though they may be. These inside movements, stirrings, or sensations may change several times an hour. They may occur in multiples, forming duets and trios that sometimes produce harmony and at other times create dissonance.[2]

There are many people today who honestly do not know how to express their emotions. They have been raised emotionally sheltered or inhibited in some way. They have lost the distinction between thinking and feeling, or they find excuses to avoid the deeper levels of conversation where emotions are verbalized.

But consider this: There is no aphrodisiac in the world as strong and powerful as an ongoing, deep level of communication that flows from one person to another. Sexual intimacy and fulfillment spring from conversational intimacy. There are no shortcuts or techniques that can substitute for honest expression of inner feelings.

Let's go a bit deeper by you and your partner each taking a sheet of paper and completing the following exercise. Do not discuss your responses until you are both finished.

1. I see myself as being emotionally open in the following manner:

   a. I throw open the door and let it all hang out.

   b. I open the door, but tend to keep my hand on the door just in case.

   c. I open the door halfway to see what happens.

   d. I open the door a crack and peek out.

   e. I use deadbolt locks and barricade the door.

   f. Where's the door?

2. I see you as being emotionally open in the following manner:

   a. You throw open the door and let it all hang out.

   b. You open the door, but tend to keep your hand on the doorknob just in case.

   c. You open the door halfway to see what happens.

   d. You open the door a crack and peek out.

   e. You use deadbolt locks and barricade the door.

   f. Do you know where the door is?

3. The emotions I have difficulty expressing openly are:

   a. fear

   b. disappointment

   c. pleasure

   d. sadness

   e. resentment

   f. hurt

   g. frustration

   h. anxiety

   i. anger

   j. joy

   k. delight

   l. elation

   m. love

4. What do you do when you have difficulty expressing one of these emotions?

5. What does your spouse do when he/she has difficulty expressing one of these emotions?

6. Which emotion is the easiest for you to express?

7. Which emotion is the easiest for your spouse to express?

For emotional intimacy to occur in this exercise, the next step is vital. Sit face-to-face with your partner (which also means knee-to-knee) and hold hands. Holding hands increases the intimacy and also tends to keep a lid on any temptation to get upset. Take turns sharing your responses with one another. You might even begin by asking your spouse how he/she feels about responding to the questions and discussing them in this manner. Be sure you conclude your time by discussing what you can do to increase the level of emotional conversation in your relationship.

EIGHT

Roles, Responsibilities, and Decision-Making

What about the question of roles and responsibilities in marriage? Who does what and why? Does he or she do it? Is it because of what the church has said? Or is it because that is the way it was done in your parents' home?

Failure to clarify the husband-wife roles in a relationship is a major cause of marital disruption. As a couple you will be involved in an almost endless number of activities and responsibilities. Each couple should discuss together and decide who is most competent to do which task. Assignment of tasks should not be made simply because of parental example, because it is expected in your social group, or because of tradition. When an individual's abilities, training, and temperament make it difficult or unnecessary to follow an established cultural norm for a role, the couple will need to have the strength to establish their own style of working together. It is imperative that a couple deliberately and mutually develop the rules and guidelines for *their* relationship as husband and wife. This clear assignment of authority and responsibility by the spouses does not create a rigid relationship but allows flexibility and order in what could become a chaotic mess.

Let's spend some time thinking about your role as a wife or husband.

A Woman's Place—Where Are You?

Property—wife has almost no rights and privileges compared to those of the husband. Husband is the family provider. Often the wife is merely a chattel for the husband's sexual expression.

Complement—wife's rights have increased. Marriage is the wife's central life interest. Husband is chief provider and has more authority than wife. She is a friend to her husband. He achieves and she supports him.

Junior Partner—wife's rights increase because she works outside the home for pay. Her main motive is to improve the family's lifestyle. She has more authority (rights) than a nonworking woman.

Equal Partner—wife and husband share equal rights and responsibilities.

On the chart below, place your initials below the mark
that indicates your vision of your spouse's role in marriage.
Then place your spouse's initials where you think he or she would.

Property   **Complement**   **Junior Partner**   **Equal Partner**

When both of you have completed your chart, share your responses. After that, complete the following sentences and discuss them.

1. In marriage I believe a role is . . .

2. My main role in marriage is . . .

3. I began to form this belief about my role when . . .

4. My mate's role is . . .

5. In marriage a wife should . . .

6. In marriage a husband should . . .

7. I can best help my mate fulfill his or her role by . . .

Use a separate piece of paper for the Role Concepts Comparison that follows. Read each statement and write the appropriate number indicating what you believe about each one. Then go back and indicate how you think your partner responded to each statement. Finally, write down where you obtained each belief—from your parents, pastor, friends, or your own idea.

Role Concepts Comparison

What do you believe about your role concept in marriage? For each statement, circle your level of belief:

1 – strongly agree
2 – mildly agree
3 – not sure
4 – mildly disagree
5 – strongly disagree

Wife   *Husband*

Wife		Statement	Husband
1 2 3 4 5	A.	The husband is the head of the home.	1 2 3 4 5
1 2 3 4 5	B.	The wife should not be employed outside the home.	1 2 3 4 5
1 2 3 4 5	C.	The husband should help regularly with the dishes.	1 2 3 4 5
1 2 3 4 5	D.	It is all right for the wife to initiate love-making.	1 2 3 4 5
1 2 3 4 5	E.	The husband and wife should plan the budget and manage money together.	1 2 3 4 5
1 2 3 4 5	F.	Neither the husband nor the wife should purchase an item costing more than $30 without consulting the other.	1 2 3 4 5
1 2 3 4 5	G.	The husband is the one responsible for disciplining the children.	1 2 3 4 5
1 2 3 4 5	H.	A wife who has special talent should have a career.	1 2 3 4 5
1 2 3 4 5	I.	It is the wife's responsibility to keep the house neat and clean.	1 2 3 4 5
1 2 3 4 5	J.	The husband should take his wife out twice a month.	1 2 3 4 5
1 2 3 4 5	K.	The wife is just as responsible for the children's discipline as the husband.	1 2 3 4 5
1 2 3 4 5	L.	It is the husband's job to do the yard work.	1 2 3 4 5

(continued on page 54)

Role Concepts Comparison

(continued from page 53)

Wife			Husband
1 2 3 4 5	**M.**	The wife should be the teacher of values to the children.	1 2 3 4 5
1 2 3 4 5	**N.**	Children should be allowed to help plan family activities.	1 2 3 4 5
1 2 3 4 5	**O.**	Children develop better in a home with parents who are strict disciplinarians.	1 2 3 4 5
1 2 3 4 5	**P.**	Money that the wife earns is her money.	1 2 3 4 5
1 2 3 4 5	**Q.**	The husband should have at least one night a week out with his friends.	1 2 3 4 5
1 2 3 4 5	**R.**	The wife should always be the one to cook.	1 2 3 4 5
1 2 3 4 5	**S.**	The husband's responsibility is to his job, and the wife's responsibility is to the home and children.	1 2 3 4 5

What does the Word of God say concerning the role of the wife and the role of the husband? Read Ephesians 5:21-33, then answer the following questions.

1. What one word summarizes a wife's responsibility to her husband? (See also 1 Peter 3:1.)

2. What do the words *as unto the Lord* in Ephesians 5:22 suggest about the wife's role?

3. Are there any limits placed upon the wife's submission by Colossians 3:18 and Acts 5:29?

4. According to Ephesians 5:33, what should the wife's attitude be toward her husband? What does this mean in everyday life?

5. What does the word *submission* mean to you? Write down a definition.

Submission does not mean that the wife is inferior, nor does it stifle her initiative. It does not limit her in any way. Read Proverbs 31:10-31. On a separate piece of paper make a list of the ways this woman in Proverbs uses her abilities.

What is the man's role in marriage. Is submission a part of his role and function? What does Ephesians 5:21 say?

1. Study Ephesians 5:22-33. What two words in this section summarize the husband's responsibility? (Compare verse 23 with verse 25; also see Philippians 2:4.)

2. What example should the husband exhibit as he leads in the marriage relationship? (Compare Ephesians 1:22 with 5:23.) In light of this, for whose benefit should the headship of the husband be exercised?

3. For whose benefit is the headship of Christ exercised? (Compare Ephesians 1:22 and 5:25-27.) For whose benefit should the headship of the husband be exercised?

4. What are the ways in which Christ loved the church? Relate each of these to the way a husband should love his wife.

5. In Proverbs we see that the wife has been given great responsibility and is able to use her gifts. What gifts or abilities does your wife have that you do not?

6. In Proverbs 31:28,29 the husband praises and expresses appreciation to his wife. Could this be the reason she is so capable?

Perhaps you are already getting the idea that in marriage each one gives to and receives from the other. Marriage is built upon each person being a complement to the other. Dr. Dwight Small expressed it this way:

When a man and a woman unite in marriage, humanity experiences a restoration to wholeness. The glory of the man is the acknowledgment that woman was created for him; the glory of the woman is the acknowledgment that man is incomplete without her; the humility of the woman is the acknowledgment that she was made for man; the humility of the man is the acknowledgment that he is incomplete without her. Both share an equal dignity, honor, and worth. Yes, and each shares a humility before the other, also. Each is nec-essarily the completion of the other; each is necessarily dependent upon the other.[1]

Earlier you probably discovered that the role of the husband is that of a servant. It is a servanthood role! What are some creative ways a husband can be a loving leader-servant?

1.

2.

3.

4.

5.

6.

7.

8.

9.

10.

Every couple directly or indirectly establishes a pattern for reaching marital decisions. Many of these patterns are ineffective or self-defeating. Some bring about lingering feelings of resentment. The majority of couples have not considered how they arrive at decisions. Have you?

1. Who made most of the decisions in your family? How would your partner answer this question?

2. Have you established guidelines to distinguish between major and minor decisions? If so, what are they?

3. What procedure do you follow when there is an impasse and a decision must be made?

4. How did you decide upon responsibilities for household chores?

5. In what areas of family life do you have the right to make decisions without consulting your spouse? Who decided this policy? How did you arrive at this decision?

6. Do you make the decisions you want to make or the ones your spouse does not want to make?

7. Do you have any veto power over your spouse's decisions? If so, what is the basis for it, and how did you arrive at this decision?

How did you do in answering these questions? Most couples have never thought them through, and yet they are vital to an understanding of the marital relationship.

Answer these questions and then compare your responses with those of your spouse.

1. I'm afraid to make decisions when . . .

2. I'm afraid to have my partner make decisions when . . .

3. I'd like to make decisions when . . .

4. I'd like my partner to make decisions when . . .

5. I want to make decisions in the area of . . .

6. I want my partner to make decisions in the area of . . .

Consider these thoughts about the roles of the husband and wife and decision-making:

The principle of mutuality of submissiveness in marriage is similar to the pattern of submissiveness between the members of the Body of Christ. There are times in the Body when it is appropriate for one member to exercise leadership over the other members as a function of his or her spiritual gift (1 Corinthians 12:14-26). No single spiritual gift automatically qualifies a member to be the leader or ultimate decision-maker all of the time. That position belongs to the head, Jesus Himself. Likewise, in a marriage in which there is mutuality of submissiveness, the role of leadership is assigned not according to some decree from God, or on the basis of "maleness" or "femaleness," but on the basis of the leadership role the partner has been assigned by the mutual decision of the marriage. The skill of a Christian marriage lies in the negotiation and assignment of these leadership roles on the basis of the abilities of the partners.[2]

In the marriage the husband has the office of head. That simply means he has the responsibility and authority to call the marriage—his wife as well as himself—to obey the norm of troth. If he faithfully exercises his office, both he and his wife will be freed to be themselves. As the head, the husband is called to take the lead in mutually examining the marriage to see if it is developing according to its long-range goals.

Clearly, headship has nothing to do with being boss. The husband can only command the wife to live up to what the two of them mutually pledged when they were married. Likewise, if the husband neglects his office, the wife ought to call the husband back to their mutual vows.

Neither does headship imply inferiority or superiority. Rather, headship is a special office of service so that the marriage may thrive and grow. Headship does not mean that the husband leads or decides in every detail. Once a man and woman have decided which vision of life is going to be the norm in their activities in their marriage, they can leave the decisions in day-to-day

affairs to the partner with the appropriate talents, temperaments, and situations. The husband's role is to be on guard continually so that the "little" things do not develop into the kinds of patterns that undermine the entire marriage.[3]

How will the presence of Jesus Christ in your life help you in the process of decision-making and discovering your gifts in marriage?

NINE

In-Laws or Outlaws?

Y ou are an in-law. What does the word in-law mean to you? Write your definition below, and share it with your partner.

What examples of in-laws do we find in the Scriptures? Read the following three selections and ask yourself, "How would I have responded if I had been in the same situation?"

1. Genesis 26:34–27:46
2. Exodus 18:13-24
3. Ruth

Describe the ideal in-law relationship from your perspective. Share this with your partner.

Describe what you think would be the ideal in-law relationship from your parents' perspective and from that of your partner's parents.

Here are 20 of the most important questions concerning in-laws. Answer them and share your responses with your spouse.

1. Genesis 2:24; Matthew 19:5; Mark 10:7,8; and Ephesians 5:31 all say the same thing. What does the word *leave* mean to you?

2. If your parents were able to help you financially in any way, what might they expect in return?

3. How do your parents feel about your partner?

4. Are there any emotional issues with your parents that interfere with your relationship? Explain.

5. How do you think your in-laws view you?

6. What would you consider interference by your in-laws?

7. How did you get along with your mother and father during your childhood?

8. Describe your present relationship with your mother and father.

9. How do you think your parents view your partner?

10. What one thing about your partner's parents do you dislike?

11. What three things about your partner's parents do you appreciate?

12. What customs in your home differ from those in your partner's home?

13. Describe how and where you like to spend your Thanksgiving and Christmas.

14. What have you done in the past to let your parents and in-laws know they are important to you?

15. During the past two weeks, what have you done to express positive feelings toward your parents and your in-laws?

16. What new things could you say or do that would let your parents and your in-laws know they are important to you?

17. Describe what you have done to discover from your parents or in-laws what kind of relationship they expect from you and your partner, how often to visit or call, their involvement in disciplining the children, and so on.

18. In the past, how have you helped your parents or in-laws meet their own needs and develop a greater meaning in life? How can you help them in the future?

19. In the next 10 to 20 years, what type of help will your parents or your spouse's parents need from you?

20. Have you discussed with your parents or in-laws what they need or want from you as they become more dependent upon you?

TEN

Communication

Communication is to love what blood is to life. Have you ever thought about it that way before? It is impossible to have any kind of relationship unless there is communication. That is true for you and your partner and for your relationship with God. Write your definition of communication, and share your answer with your partner.

Now define *listening* and share your definition.

If there is any indispensable insight with which a young married couple should begin their life together, it is that they should try to keep open, at all cost, the lines of communication between them.[1]

A marriage can be likened to a large house with many rooms to which a couple fall heir on their wedding day. Their hope

is to use and enjoy these rooms, as we do the rooms in a comfortable home, so that they will serve the many activities that make up their shared life. But in many marriages, doors are found to be locked—they represent areas in the relationship which the couple are unable to explore together. Attempts to open these doors lead to failure and frustration. The right key cannot be found. So the couple resign themselves to living together in only a few rooms that can be opened easily, leaving the rest of the house, with all its promising possibilities, unexplored and unused.

There is, however, a master key that will open every door. It is not easy to find. Or, more correctly, it has to be forged by the couple together, and this can be very difficult. It is the great art of effective marital communication.[2]

Let's consider another aspect of communication. In our communication we send messages. Every message has three components: the actual content, the tone of the voice, and the nonverbal communication. With changes in the tone of voice or in the nonverbal component, it is possible to express many different messages using the same words, statements, or questions. Nonverbal communication includes facial expression, body posture, and actions. An example of nonverbal communication that should be avoided is holding a book or newspaper in front of one's face while talking.

The three components of communication must be complementary. One researcher has suggested the following breakdown of the importance of the three components.[3] The percentages indicate how much of the message is sent through each one.

Content	7%
Tone	38%
Nonverbal	55%

Confusing messages are often sent because the three components contradict one another. Take a minute and think about how you communicate nonverbally. Then write how your partner communicates nonverbally. After you have done this, write what you think your nonverbal communication means to the other person and what you think your partner's nonverbal communication means. Ask your spouse to do this too, and then compare and discuss your responses.

Our nonverbal communication and tone of voice are essential elements in conveying our messages. If you are not aware of your tone of voice, you may want to use a tape recorder to record some of your conversations. Play them back and pay attention to your tone of voice and what it implies.

How will you communicate in the following situations?

1. It's Saturday. Your spouse asks you to shop for something but you really don't want to go. You say:

2. You are trying to watch your favorite TV program but your spouse is continually interrupting and asking you questions. The program is at a crucial part, and you don't want to miss it. You say:

3. You are describing to your spouse the most exciting event of the day. Right in the middle of it your spouse yawns and says, "I think I'll go get a cup of coffee." You say:

4. Your spouse serves you breakfast. You notice that the bacon is overcooked, which you don't like. The toast is served lightly toasted with fresh butter, which is exactly what you like. You say:

5. After dinner your spouse asks you if you would do the dishes tonight because he or she is so tired. You, too, are tired and were looking forward to relaxing. Usually you both do them together. You say:

6. You have just had an argument with one of your children and you realize you are wrong. It is not easy to apologize to family members because they usually rub it in. You say:

What does the Word of God say about communication? Look up the passages listed and write the key thought for each one. You will notice that the verses are listed in groupings because there is a central theme in each group. See if you can discover the central thought for each group and write it as a summary.

1. Proverbs 11:9
   Proverbs 12:18
   Proverbs 15:4
   Proverbs 18:8
   Proverbs 18:21
   Proverbs 25:11
   Proverbs 26:22
   James 3:8-10
   1 Peter 3:10
   Summary:

2. Proverbs 4:20-23
   Proverbs 6:12,14,18
   Proverbs 15:28
   Proverbs 16:2
   Proverbs 16:23
   Summary:

3. Proverbs 15:31
   Proverbs 18:13
   Proverbs 18:15
   Proverbs 19:20
   Proverbs 21:28
   James 1:19
   Summary:

4. Proverbs 12:18
   Proverbs 14:29
   Proverbs 15:28

Proverbs 16:32
Proverbs 21:23
Proverbs 26:4
Proverbs 29:20
Summary:

5. Proverbs 15:23
   Proverbs 25:11
   Summary:

6. Proverbs 10:19
   Proverbs 11:12,13
   Proverbs 13:3
   Proverbs 17:27,28
   Proverbs 18:2
   Proverbs 20:19
   Proverbs 21:23
   Summary:

7. Proverbs 17:9
   Proverbs 21:9
   Summary:

8. Proverbs 15:1
   Proverbs 15:4
   Proverbs 16:1
   Proverbs 25:15
   Summary:

9. Proverbs 12:16
   Proverbs 19:11
   Summary:

10. Proverbs 12:17,22
    Proverbs 16:13
    Proverbs 19:5
    Proverbs 26:18,19
    Proverbs 26:22
    Proverbs 28:23
    Proverbs 29:5
    Ephesians 4:15,25
    Colossians 3:9
    Summary:

Let's see what kind of communicator you are and discover how much you know about your spouse. Assume that you are interviewing a stranger. Your task is to ask the other person any question you want about marriage, dating experiences, childhood, hobbies, likes and dislikes, religious views, self-image, looks, and so on. Keep in mind that you know nothing about the other person. Construct your questions so that you assume nothing. Keep your opinions out. When you have completed the interview, change roles and have your partner interview you.

In his book *Why Am I Afraid to Tell You Who I Am?* John Powell states that we communicate on five different levels, from shallow clichés to deep personal comments. Hang-ups, such as fear, apathy, or a poor self-image keep us at the shallow level. If we can be freed from our restric-

tions, we can move to the deeper more meaningful level. What are the five levels of communication?

Level Five: Cliché conversation. This type of talk is very safe. We use phrases such as "How are you?" "How's the dog?" "Where have you been?" "I like your dress." In this type of conversation there is no personal sharing. Each person remains safely behind his or her defenses.

Level Four: Reporting the facts about others. In this kind of conversation we are content to tell others what someone else has said, but we offer no personal information on these facts. We report the facts like the six o'clock news. We share gossip and little narrations, but we do not commit ourselves to how we feel about them.

Level Three: My ideals and judgments. Real communication begins to unfold here. We are willing to step out of our solitary confinements and risk telling some of our ideas and decisions. We are still cautious. If we sense that what we are saying is not being accepted, we will retreat.

Level Two: My feelings or emotions. At this level we share how we feel about facts, ideas, and judgments. Our feelings underneath these areas are revealed. For us to really share ourselves with other individuals, we must move to the level of sharing our feelings.

Level One: Complete emotional and personal communication. All deep relationships must be based on absolute openness and honesty. This may be difficult to achieve because it involves risk—the risk of being rejected. But it is vital if relationships are to grow. There will be times when this type of communication is not as complete as it could be.[4]

Take the time right now and write down your answer to these questions.

1. What are some of the reasons why a person might respond only at level five or level four?

2. When do you feel most like responding at levels two and one?

3. At what level do you usually respond?

4. At what level does your partner usually respond?

5. On which level do you usually share with God?

6. Describe a time when you really felt you communicated with God.

Persons who communicate primarily on a cognitive or thinking level deal mainly with factual data. They like to talk about such topics as sports, the stock market, money, house, and jobs. They keep the subject of conversation out of the emotional arena. Usually they are quite uncomfortable dealing with issues that elicit feelings, especially unpleasant feelings such as anger. Consequently they avoid talking about subjects that involve love, fear, and anger. These people have difficulty being warm and supportive of their spouses.

Others communicate more on the feeling level. They tire easily of purely factual data and feel a need to share feelings, especially with their spouses. They feel that the atmosphere between husband and wife must be as free as possible from unpleasant feelings like tension, anger, and resentment. So, of course, they want to talk about these emotional things, resolve conflicts with their spouses, clear the air, and keep things pleasant between them.

Of course no one is completely cognitive or completely emotional. Where are you and where is your spouse? On the diagram below indicate: 1) where you think you are; 2) where you think your partner is, and 3) where you think your mate would place you.

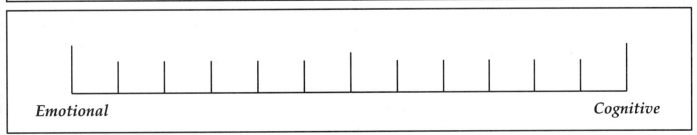

Emotional   Cognitive

A person on the left side of the graph, who shares more feelings, is not less bright or less intellectual. This person is simply aware of his/her feelings and is usually better able to do something about them.

A surprising fact is that the "cognitive" person (on the right) is controlled by his/her feelings just as the "emotional" person is, but he/she doesn't realize it. For example, the stiff, formal intellectual has deep feelings but uses enormous energy to keep them buried so they won't interfere with daily life. Unfortunately they do. Whenever someone (like an "emotional" spouse or child) is around asking for affection and warmth, he/she is not only unable to respond, but is also angered that his/her precious equilibrium has been disturbed.[5]

Communication is the process of sharing yourself verbally and nonverbally in such a way that the other person can both accept and understand what you are sharing. Listening is also a vital tool for communication.

What is listening? Paul Tournier said, "How beautiful, how grand and liberating this experience is, when people learn to help each other. It is impossible to overemphasize the immense need humans have to be really listened to. Listen to all the conversations of our world, between nations as well as those between couples. They are, for the most part, dialogues of the deaf."[6]

The Living Bible expresses these thoughts about listening: "Any story sounds true until someone tells the other side and sets the record straight" (Proverbs 18:17). "The wise man learns by listening; the simpleton can learn only by seeing scorners punished" (Proverbs 21:11). The Amplified Bible tells us "He who answers a matter before he hears the facts, it is folly and shame to him" (Proverbs 18:13). "Let every man be quick to hear, (a ready listener)..." (James 1:19, AMP).

What do we mean by listening? When we are listening to another person we are not thinking about what we are going to say when he/she stops talking. We are not busy formulating our response. We are concentrating on what is being said. Listening is also complete acceptance without judgment of what is said or how it is said. Often we fail to hear the message because we don't like it or the tone of voice. We react and miss the meaning of what was being shared.

Acceptance doesn't mean you have to agree with everything being said. Acceptance means you understand that what the other person is saying is something he/she feels. Real listening means we should be able to repeat what the other person has said and what we thought he/she was feeling when speaking to us.

It is important to become very proficient in communication. You may want to read *How to Speak Your Spouse's Language* (Revell Publishers) by H. Norman Wright.

ELEVEN

Conflict (or "Sound the Battle Cry!")

Did you anticipate conflict in your marriage? If not, you probably were in for a surprise. Conflict is a fact of life. It has been defined as a slash, contention, or sharp disagreement over interests, ideas, and so forth. Why does it occur? The answer is simply that we are human beings—imperfect people whom God graciously loves in spite of our imperfections. All of us have our own desires, wants, needs, and goals. Whenever any of these differ from another, conflict may occur. Our differences in beliefs, ideas, attitudes, feelings, and behavior vary. The conflicts themselves are not the problem, but our reaction to them is.

Many times disagreements or conflicts do not need to be completely resolved. An example may be a disagreement over political philosophy. This type of disagreement could continue indefinitely and need not destroy the overall marital relationship.

1. What does "completely resolved" mean to you?

2. List some of the issues you and your partner disagree on that do not need to be completely resolved.

3. Make a list of some issues on which you disagree that do need solutions—that more time needs to be spent on exploring alternatives.

4. Select one of the issues on which more time needs to be spent. Write an explanation of the situation as you see it.

5. Some people have learned to use weapons in dealing with conflict. What are some unfair weapons?

6. What effect does anger have on finding solutions to conflict? What effect does anger have on marriage?

Remember that anger comes about for three basic reasons: hurt, fear, and frustration. (If you would like to explore this topic further, read *Winning Over Your Emotions* by H. Norman Wright [Harvest House].)

What do the following verses have to say about the right way to handle anger?

1. Psalm 37:1-11

2. Proverbs 14:29

3. Proverbs 15:1

4. Proverbs 15:28

5. Proverbs 16:32

6. Proverbs 19:11

7. Proverbs 25:28

8. Proverbs 29:11

9. Matthew 5:43,44

10. Romans 8:28,29

11. Romans 12:19,21

12. Galatians 5:16-23

13. Ephesians 4:26

14. Ephesians 4:29

15. Ephesians 4:32

16. 1 Peter 3:9

A look at your relationship

What causes conflicts? (Read James 4:1-3.)

1. Describe a recent or current conflict between you and your partner.

2. What do you believe caused the conflict? What was the outcome? What did it accomplish?

3. How did you create or contribute to the conflict?

4. Imagine that you are seeing the conflict from the other person's perspective. How would your partner describe the conflict?

5. If you could go through the same conflict again, how would you handle it?

```
         YIELD                    RESOLVE

                   COMPROMISE

         WITHDRAW                 WIN
```

Remember this: Conflict is a natural part of growth and family living. Many conflicts are simply symptoms of something else. Most people do not deal openly with conflict because no one has ever taught them effective ways of dealing with it. Unresolved and buried conflicts arise from their grave and interfere with growth and satisfying relationships. On the positive side, conflict does provide opportunities for growth in a relationship.

What choices do we have in dealing with conflicts? James Fairfield has suggested five styles of dealing with conflict.[1]

The first is to withdraw. If you have a tendency to view conflict as a hopeless inevitability that you can do little to control, you may not even try. You may withdraw physically by leaving the scene or you may leave psychologically.

If you feel you must always look after your own interests or your self-concept is threatened in a conflict, you may choose to win. No matter what the cost, you must win! Domination is usually reflected in this style; personal relationships take second place.

While driving along the highway or approaching an intersection you have probably noticed a yield sign. "Giving in to get along" is another style of handling conflict. You don't like it, but rather than risk a confrontation you choose this path.

"Give a little to get a little" is called compromise. You may find that it is important to let up on some of your demands or ideas in order to help the other person give a little. You don't want to win all the time, nor do you want the other person to win all the time.

A person may choose to resolve conflicts. In this style of dealing with conflicts, situations, attitudes, or behaviors are changed by open and direct communication.

1. Which of these is your usual style of dealing with conflicts?

2. What is your partner's usual style?

3. Describe a situation in which you withdrew from a conflict.

4. Describe a situation in which you won a conflict.

5. Describe a situation in which you yielded in a conflict.

6. Describe a situation in which you compromised in a conflict.

7. Describe a situation in which you resolved a conflict.

8. Describe how each solution affected the feelings of others toward you.

Withdrew:

Won:

Yielded:

Compromised:

Resolved:

9. How did you feel about yourself in each situation?

Withdrew:

Won:

Yielded:

Compromised:

Resolved:

10. Did the results eventually bring about a more peaceful atmosphere in each case?

What style did Jesus use? Take a few minutes and read the following accounts of conflict. Try to determine the methods used at that time. Write down the various styles you observe.

1. Matthew 15:10-20

2. Mark 11:11-19

High concern for relationship

YIELD	RESOLVE
	COMPROMISE
WITHDRAW	WIN

Low in achieved needs

High in achieved needs

Low concern for relationship

---

3. Luke 23:18-49

4. John 8:1-11

5. John 11:11-19

You may ask "Which style is best?" "Which is best for our marriage?"

As you can see from the diagram above, *withdraw* has the lowest value because the person gives up on meeting the goals and developing the relationship. The relationship is turned off. If this style is used temporarily as a cooling off step toward

resolve, it is beneficial. There may be times when the discussion is so heated and out of control that withdrawing is best. But it is important to make a definite and specific commitment to discuss and resolve the conflict.

The *win* method achieves the goal but can sacrifice the relationship. In a family, personal relationships are just as important or more important than the goal.

Yielding works just the other way in that the goals are sacrificed.

Compromise attempts to work out some needs, but the bargaining involved may mean you compromise some of your own values. If you have some basic convictions about the type of young people your daughter or son dates and you begin to compromise your standards in order to have greater harmony, what does that do to you?

Naturally the highest value or style is *resolve* because, in the final analysis, relationships are strengthened as you seek to meet personal needs.

How then can we resolve conflicts? Consider trying and applying these principles that a couple developed for their relationship. They put it in the form of a covenant. You may want to create your own covenant.

Communication Covenant

This covenant will be read together each Sunday, and then we will ask one another in what way can we improve our application of this covenant in our daily life.

1. We will express irritations and annoyances we have with one another in a loving, specific, and positive way rather than holding them in or being negative in general.

    a. I will acknowledge that I have a problem rather than stating you are doing such and such.

    b. I will not procrastinate by waiting for the right time to express irritations or annoyances.

    c. I will pinpoint to myself the reason for my annoyances. I will ask myself why I feel irritation or annoyance over this problem.

2. We will not exaggerate or attack the other person during the course of a disagreement.

    a. I will stick with the specific issue.

    b. I will take several seconds to formulate my words so that I can be accurate.

    c. I will consider the consequences of what I say before I say it.

    d. I will not use the words *always, all the time, everyone, nothing,* etc.

3. We will attempt to control the emotional level and intensity of arguments (no yelling, uncontrollable anger, hurtfulness).

    a. We will take time-outs for calming down if either of us feels that our own anger is starting to elevate too much. The minimum amount of time for a time-out will be one minute and the maximum, ten minutes. The person who needs a greater amount of time in order to calm down will be the one to set the time limit. During the time-out each person, in writing, will first of all define the problem that is being discussed. Second, the areas of agreement in the problem will be listed. Third, the areas of disagreement will be listed, and fourth, three alternate solutions to this problem will be listed. When we come back together the person who has been the most upset will express to the other individual, "I'm interested in what you've written during our time-out. Will you share yours with me?"

    b. Before I say anything, I will decide if I would want this same statement said to me with the same words and tone of voice.

4. We will "never let the sun go down on our anger" or never run away from each other during an argument.

    a. I will remind myself that controlling my emotional level will get things resolved quicker and make one less inclined to back off from the problem.

    b. I am willing to make a personal sacrifice.

    c. I will not take advantage of my mate by drawing out the discussion. If we have discussed an issue for 15 minutes, then at that time we will take a time-out and put into practice the written procedure discussed under #3.

5. We will both try hard not to interrupt the other person when he/she is talking (as

a result of this commitment, there will be no need to keep reminding the other person of his/her responsibility, especially during an argument).

    a. I will consider information that will be lost by interrupting the other person.

    b. It is important that the person talking should be concise and to the point.

    c. I will remember that the person who was interrupted won't be able to listen as well as possible if I had waited for my turn.

    d. I will put into practice Proverbs 18:13 and James 1:19.

6. We will carefully listen to the other person when he/she is talking (rather than spending that time thinking up a defense).

    a. If I find myself formulating my response while the other person is talking, I will say, "Please stop and repeat what you said because I was not listening, and I want to hear what you were sharing."

    b. If we are having difficulty hearing one another, then when a statement is made, we will repeat back to the other person what we heard and what we thought he/she was feeling.

7. We will not toss in past failures of the other person in the course of an argument.

    a. I will remind myself that a past failure has been discussed and forgiven. True forgiveness means it will not be brought up to the person again.

    b. I will remind myself that bringing up a past failure cripples the other person from growing and developing.

    c. If I catch myself bringing up a past failure, I will ask the other person's forgiveness. Then I will state what it is that I am desirous that the other person will do in the future, and I will commit myself to this behavior.

8. When something is important enough for one person to discuss, it is that important for the other person.

    a. If I have difficulty wanting to discuss what the other person desires to discuss, I will say, "I know this topic is important to you, and I do want to hear this even though it is a bit difficult for me."

    b. In implementing this agreement and all the principles of communication in this covenant we will eliminate outside interferences to our communication such as the radio on, television, reading books on our lap, etc. We will look at one another and hold hands during our discussion times.

Date _____

Husband's
signature_____

Wife's
signature _____

TWELVE

Finances

❧

Money! It takes money to pay the rent, the tax collector, and the utility companies. Your attitude toward money and your past lifestyle may have needed an adjustment when you married. Financial disruption and difficulties can place a tremendous strain upon the marital relationship. The next several sections have been designed to help you determine what is important to you in terms of finances and help you make some realistic plans.

Study the following passages to discover how to acquire, how to regard, and how to spend money. Indicate the principles that you derive from each passage.

1. Deuteronomy 8:17,18

2. 1 Chronicles 29:11,12

3. Proverbs 11:24,25

4. Proverbs 11:28

5. Proverbs 12:10

6. Proverbs 13:11; 14:23

7. Proverbs 13:18,22

8. Proverbs 15:6

9. Proverbs 15:16,17,22

10. Proverbs 15:27

11. Proverbs 16:8	23. Ecclesiastes 5:19
12. Proverbs 16:16	24. Matthew 6:19,20
13. Proverbs 20:4,14,18	25. Matthew 17:24-27
14. Proverbs 21:5,6	26. Luke 6:27-38
15. Proverbs 21:20,25,26	27. Luke 12:13-21
16. Proverbs 22:1,4,7	28. Romans 13:6-8
17. Proverbs 23:1-5	29. Ephesians 4:28
18. Proverbs 24:30-34	30. Philippians 4:11-19
19. Proverbs 27:23,24	31. 2 Thessalonians 3:7-12
20. Proverbs 28:6,22	32. 1 Timothy 6:6-10
21. Proverbs 30:24,25	33. 1 Timothy 6:17-19
22. Ecclesiastes 5:10	34. Hebrews 13:5

Do's and Don'ts for Budgeting

1. Plan together. Hold a definite date together to seek agreement and cooperation. Make decisions together. Figures and plans should be known by all.

2. Define your financial goals. Launch your budget with a purpose in mind. Have a clear idea of why you're trying to budget.

3. Don't rush into a budget before you know how much you now spend for what. Devote several weeks to keeping a detailed expense record for use in working on a budget. If you do not know where your money is going, you cannot sensibly decide where it should go.

4. Do not think up countless budget headings. Use common sense in approaching, clarifying, and classifying according to your family's spending habits.

5. Divvy up your dollars according to the family's needs and wants. Do not allocate according to the way other people spend. Use averages—canned guides and other outside advice—as rough starting points only. Indicate your specific needs and wants:

Needs	Cost

Wants	Cost

6. Think first. When allocating, trimming, or adjusting budget amounts, do not jump to conclusions. Do not let wishful thinking take the place of sober appraisal. Does an expense item look too high? Find out whether it really is high, or why it is high, before cutting it. If you are looking for a place to economize so you can spend more on something else, do not cut any old thing arbitrarily. Before you do whittle down an item, spell out precisely what specific items of past expenditures are to be reduced or eliminated.

7. Plan for the big expenses. You can expect several big, nonrecurring expenses during the year: taxes, insurance, vacation bills, and so on. Forecast—lay aside an amount each month to meet these expenses when they come due. If not planned for, a few of these dropped smack into regular, month-to-month expenses will throw your budget into a chaos from which it may never recover.

8. Know who is in charge of what. Each member of the family should know just what his or her responsibilities are.

9. Do not keep track of every penny. Family members should be allowed to spend their allowances as they choose, without having to make an entry in the budget. Do not insist that everyone keep itemized lists of all expenses. Do not demand detailed accounts and summaries.

10. Do not intermingle funds. Do have a clear-cut system for divvying up the paycheck. A checking account is a good system. You deposit a sum of money each payday to cover expenses, keeping record of how much is earmarked for what. This way you will not be spending more than you have allotted for any one budget item.

11. Do not cheat your budget. For example, if your budgeting shows you cannot afford a new ski outfit this month, do not go out and charge it. A debt like this should always be taken into account for next month's planning. Otherwise, you will find a substantial amount of your funds has already been spent, thanks to the charge.

12. When the budget starts to rub tight, let it out here, tuck it in there, to give a better fit. Do not keep it ironclad and inflexible. A grim, unbending budget will soon make everybody sullen, if not outright mutinous. A good rule of evaluation is to look at your budget every January and every July to make sure it is realistic and working for your benefit.

And . . . do not quit the first chance you get. Budgets seldom click the first time around. Hang on, start revising, try fresh starts. Do not toss in the towel. If at first you don't succeed, you know what to do!

As you make out your budget be sure to insert an item designated "Marriage Enrichment." This amount, which could be from $50 to $250 per year, is set aside for you to use for the enhancement of your marriage. It can be used for books to read together, tapes to listen to together, honeymoon weekends, and marriage enrichment retreats. By doing this, and planning this as a goal, you should be able to build the quality of married life that you are both seeking at this time. But it doesn't just happen. It takes planning and work.

How will the presence of Jesus Christ in your life help you with the financial aspect of your married life?

Making the Budget Work

In making a budget work for you it is important that both partners decide and agree together.

After taking out all the taxes from your paycheck you are left with X amount of dollars. From that you also deduct your church tithe, pledge, or offering. For the sake of simple illustration, let us say that your gross earnings are $2500, taxes amount to $600, and you are tithing $200. You are then left with $1700 of usable income, which is broken down in the following manner:

10% = $170: Savings for investment for retirement (never to be spent until retirement)

75% = $1275: For living expenses:
  housing (mortgage or rent)
  food
  insurance (car, health, etc.)
  clothes
  utilities (water, gas, phone, electricity, etc.)
  car maintenance (gas, repairs, etc.)
  magazine subscriptions, etc.

15% = $255: To clear present debts and accounts charging interest, then this can be used to save for major purchases (dishwasher, vacations, etc.) and emergencies

Now, here is some space for you to figure out your own finances:

Gross earnings _____

Subtract taxes and
all withholding — _____

Subtotal _____

Subtract tithe,
pledge, or offering — _____

Usable income _____

10% of usable income: _____

75% of usable income: _____

15% of usable income: _____

In our society it is very easy to live beyond our income. Things are nice to have, but one of the biggest blessings you can experience in a marriage is living with a little less and living close to debt-free.

Savings are a must so invest that 10 percent for good returns and do not spend the money on anything but investments. Use the 75 percent to meet your living needs—it can be done! What you have left over, the 15 percent, you need to use to clear out those credit card charges. Then use the 15 percent as an accumulating fund to pay cash for your wants, even if it takes a little time to save up.

Rate yourself on your money from the following questions: 1) definitely no; 5) definitely yes.

1. Do you have the approximate income at this time you envisioned you would?

    1   2   3   4   5

2. How do you feel about the amount of money you make?

    1   2   3   4   5

3. If your income were doubled, how would that affect your life?

    1   2   3   4   5

4. If your income were cut in half, how would that affect your life?

    1   2   3   4   5

5. Are you able to afford the things you want to buy most of the time?

    1   2   3   4   5

6. Do you and your spouse tend to agree about money issues?

    1   2   3   4   5

If 3 or less, describe what it would take to agree.

7. Do you save at least 5 percent of your income every year?

    1   2   3   4   5

8. Are you able to spend a reasonable amount of money on yourself?

    1   2   3   4   5

9. If you both are employed and one makes considerably more than the other, is this a source of conflict?

    1   2   3   4   5

10. Do you have a household budget that you adhere to each month?

    1   2   3   4   5

Family Financial Background

1. Which of these describes how you felt about money as you were growing up?

   I always felt secure that there would be enough money for whatever I needed and wanted.

   I never felt certain my parents would have enough money to give me what I wanted or needed.

   I always felt I had less than my friends had.

   I felt the people around me placed too much importance on money.

   I was embarrassed by being seen as a "rich kid."

   I knew I wanted to grow up and have a lot of money.

   Other:

2. Which of these describes how you think your spouse felt about money as he or she was growing up?

   My spouse always felt secure that there would be enough money to cover needs and wants.

   My spouse never felt certain there would be enough money to cover needs and wants.

   My spouse always felt he or she had less money than his/her friends had.

   My spouse felt that the people around him or her placed too much importance on money.

   My spouse was embarrassed by being seen as a "rich kid."

   My spouse knew he or she wanted to grow up and have a lot of money.

   Other:

3. How do these patterns affect your marriage?

4. Do you prepare your income tax well in advance, or do you wait until the last minute, rushing to the post office late on April 15?

5. If your partner prepares the tax returns, when was the last time you read one to know exactly what was earned?

6. Do you know the exact amount of each bank account?

7. Do you have all accounts listed with other important information so they're readily available to your next of kin in case of an emergency?

Do your answers indicate you may need to make some changes in your financial planning? If so, sit down and discuss it together.

THIRTEEN

Sex in Marriage

*I*n marriage, sex is supposed to grow and bloom into the best of intimate physical communication. And in some marriages the sexual relationship is getting better every day. But there are other marriages where sexual expressions (and not just intercourse) have become ruts of routine or nonexistent. The Bible talks about three specific purposes for human sexual communication.

Discovering Intimacy's Purpose

Look into what God's Word says about physical intimacy by reading the following Bible verses and talking over the discussion questions.

Procreation

Read Genesis 1:28 and Deuteronomy 7:13,14. What evidence do these verses give that sexual activity for reproduction of the human race is part of God's design?

Recreation and Release

Read Song of Solomon 4:10-12 and Proverbs 5:18,19. Does it surprise or shock you that the Scriptures actually encourage the enjoyment and sensual delights of sex?

Read Psalm 127:3 and Psalm 139:13-15 from The Living Bible. What attitude toward human sexuality and reproduction do you discover in these verses?

Reread Proverbs 5:18,19, remembering that the writer used poetic language as he spoke of sexual energies, drives, and outlets. Throughout the Bible a favorite symbol for sex is water—fountains, streams, cisterns, springs, wells, and so on. Do you agree or disagree that Proverbs 5:18,19 encourages a husband and wife to come to their bed to experience sexual pleasure? Write down your reasons:

Communication

Read Genesis 2:24. Ideally, the "one flesh" spoken of in this verse means a blending of spirit, mind, and soul—the entire being—with your spouse. Read the following paragraph that more fully describes the concepts of "one flesh," then answer the questions.

In the plan of God, sex was intended to provide a means of totally revealing oneself to the beloved, of pouring one's energies and deepest affection, hopes, and dreams into the loved one. Sex provides a means of presenting one's spouse with the gift of oneself and experiencing a like gift in return. It's a way to say "I love you." In short, sex becomes a mode of communication, a means of "knowing" each other. So, how do everyday experiences affect sexual closeness and communication? How can they affect a husband's or a wife's ability to give to the other?

1. What was the first question about sex you can remember asking your parents? How did they respond?

2. From what source (parents, friends, books) did you first learn the basic facts (or rumors) about reproduction? Can you remember anything about how you felt when you received this information?

3. When you were growing up did you have anyone with whom you felt comfortable asking questions and talking about sex? Who was it? What made that person easy to talk with?

4. The word sex means . . .

5. In marriage, sex is . . .

6. Agree or disagree: Men are "girl watchers," women are normally not "man watchers."

7. How do you respond if another person is attracted to you and approaches you?

8. What will you do if you find yourself attracted to another person?

9. How important is sex in a Christian marriage?

10. What difference would being Christians make in a couple's sexual relationship in marriage?

Our Sexual Experiences

Initiation

1. What kinds of things tend to stimulate you sexually (get you "turned on")?

2. Describe a typical process of initiation of sexual intercourse for you and your spouse (who does what, how does the other respond, etc.).

3. What about the process of initiation in your sexual relationship would you like to change?

Pleasuring

1. What kind of sexual stimulation by your partner is most pleasurable for you? Describe the kind of touch, places, length of time, and so forth.

2. Where in your body do you feel the most intense sexual sensations during sexual pleasuring?

3. Describe your feelings during this phase of a typical sexual experience for you and your spouse (include the process of bringing your worlds together, entry, and enjoying the process).

Responding—"Letting Go"

1. Describe what the sensations of sexual release are like for you. If you do not experience sexual release, try to describe at what point your feelings start to wane and what happens then.

Relaxing—Affirming

1. What do you usually do and feel during this time?

2. What do you sense from your partner at this time?

3. How might you be more affirming to your partner during the relaxation phase?

The material in this section on sexuality is simply an introduction. It is very important that you be fully informed of both physiological and biblical facts concerning sex. The vast majority of individuals are not nearly as informed as they could be, and surprisingly, women are more informed in most cases than men. It would be most beneficial to listen to the cassette series "Sex Problems and Sex Techniques in Marriage" by Dr. Ed Wheat, or you could read *Celebration of Sex* (Thomas Nelson) by Douglas Rosenau.

FOURTEEN

Your Spiritual Life Together

Spiritual intimacy is you and your partner's heart desire to be close to God and submit to His direction. It is your willingness to seek His guidance together, to allow the teaching of His Word in your everyday lives. It's a willingness to allow God to help you overcome your discomfort over sharing spiritually and help you learn to see your marriage as a spiritual adventure. It's a willingness to enthrone Jesus Christ as Lord of your lives and to look to Him for direction in your decisions, such as what house to buy, where to go on vacations, or which school is best for the children. It means God will direct both of you, and He will change your hearts to be in agreement rather than speak just through one of you.

Lordship and Control

Spiritual intimacy in marriage requires both partners to submit to the leadership and lordship of Christ, instead of competing for control. One author wrote:

We can gather all facts needed in making a decision. We can thresh out our differences as to the shape and direction our decision should take. We can put off the decision while we allow the relevant information to simmer in our minds. Even then, however, we may be uneasy; we still don't know what is best to do, and the right decision just won't come.

When we turn to the Lord Jesus Christ and open our consciences to His Spirit's leading, some new events, remembrances, and forgotten facts will come to us. A whole new pattern will emerge. We can then move with abandon in a whole new direction which we had not previously considered. Looking back, we may conclude that God's providence delivered us from what would have been the worst possible decision. Jesus as Lord made the difference between deliverance and destruction.[1]

For a couple to have spiritual intimacy they need shared beliefs as to who Jesus is and the basic tenets of the Christian faith. You may have different beliefs about the second coming of Christ or whether all the spiritual gifts are for today. One of you may enjoy an informal church service while the other likes a high-church formal service. One of you may be charismatic and the other not. *There can still be spiritual intimacy within this diversity!*

Everyone has heard about mismatched couples—one partner is a Christian, the other is not. You can also have a mismatch when both are believers but one wants to grow, and is growing, and the other doesn't and isn't.[2] A wonderful way to encourage spiritual intimacy is to share the history of your spiritual life. Many couples know where their spouses are currently, but very little of how they came to that place. Use the following questions to discover more about your partner's faith.

1. What did your parents believe about God, Jesus, church, prayer, the Bible?

2. What was your definition of being spiritually alive?

3. Which parent did you see as being spiritually alive?

4. What specifically did each teach you, directly and indirectly, about spiritual matters?

5. Where did you first learn about God? About Jesus? About the Holy Spirit? At what age?

6. What was your best experience in church as a child? As a teen?

7. What was your worst experience in church as a child? As a teen?

8. Describe your conversion experience. When was it? Who was involved? Where did it take place?

9. Describe your baptism. What did it mean to you?

10. Which Sunday school teacher influenced you the most? In what way?

11. Which minister influenced you the most? In what way?

12. What questions did you have as a child or teen about your faith? Who gave you the answers?

13. Was there any camp or special meeting that affected you spiritually?

14. Did you read the Bible as a teen?

15. Did you memorize any Scripture as a child or teen? Do you remember any now?

16. As a child, if you could have asked God any questions, what would they have been?

17. As a teen, if you could have asked God any questions, what would they have been?

18. If you could ask God any questions now, what would they be?

19. What would have helped you spiritually when you were growing up?

20. Did anyone disappoint you spiritually as a child? If so, how has that impacted you as an adult?

21. When you went through difficult times as a child or teen, how did that affect your faith?

22. What has been the greatest spiritual experience of your life?

23. When you pray, what do you pray about?

24. During marriage do you want to pray together? If so, how often?

25. Do you want to read a devotional together or separately?

26. How frequently do you want to attend church?

27. How do you see you and your spouse serving Christ together?

You may want to begin sharing God's Word and devotions together at this time. *Quiet Times for Couples* (Harvest House) provides daily readings for married couples. When children come along, *Quiet Times for Parents* (Harvest House) is an encyclopedia of parenting information. These are authored by H. Norman Wright. Two other helpful books to strengthen your relationship are *Praying God's Will for My Marriage* (Thomas Nelson) by Les Roberts and *Praying with the One You Love* (Questar) by Art Hunt.

A Closing Thought

An important principle in your marriage is to concentrate on what you will be doing either differently or positively. Then commit it to prayer—don't attempt to do it without the Lord's guidance and power. When you visualize your intent to be different or loving or accepting, you move toward that reality.

Perhaps it would be helpful to look at your marriage now, after working through this book, and consider what you like about your relationship and what you would like to see continue. Talk together about what you can do to ensure that the positive does continue.

As you can see, everything suggested in this book is simple, not at all profound. Over the years I've wondered why more couples don't follow these principles. As one husband put it, "I just never thought about it like that before. Now that I do, it makes sense." I think the potential for what can happen is summarized in this poem:

> I will be with you
> no matter what happens
> to us and between us.
> If you should become blind tomorrow,
> I will be there.
> If you achieve no success
> and attain no status in our society,
> I will be there.
>
> When we argue and are angry,
> as we inevitably will,
> I will work to bring us together.
> When we seem totally at odds
> and neither of us is having needs fulfilled,
> I will persist in trying to understand
> and in trying to restore our relationship.
>
> When our marriage seems utterly sterile
> and going nowhere at all,
> I will believe that it can work,
> and I will want it to work,
> and I will do my part to make it work.
>
> And when all is wonderful
> and we are happy,
> I will rejoice over our life together,
> and continue to strive
> to keep our relationship growing and strong.[1]

References

Notes

Chapter 1: What Is Marriage?

1. H. Norman Wright. *Secrets of a Lasting Marriage* (Ventura, CA: Regal Books, 1995).

Chapter 3: Uniqueness and Acceptance in Marriage

1. James G.T. Fairfield, *When You Don't Agree: A Guide to Resolving Marriage and Family Conflict* (Scottdale, PA: Herald Press, 1977), p. 195.

Chapter 4: Love as a Basis for Marriage

1. Leo F. Buscaglia, *Loving Each Other* (New York: Random House, Fawcett Columbine, 1984), pp. 46-50.
2. H. Norman Wright, *Holding On to Romance* (Ventura, CA: Regal Books, 1992), pp. 80-81.
3. William J. Lederer, *Marital Choices* (New York: W.W. Norton and Co., 1981), pp. 62, 63.

Chapter 5: What Did You Expect?

1. Paul Welter, *Family Problems and Predicaments* (Wheaton, IL: Tyndale House, 1977), p. 101.

Chapter 7: Fulfilling Intimacy Needs

1. Adapted from David L. Leucke, *The Relationship Manual* (Columbia, MD: The Relationship Institute, 1981), p. 25.
2. Ed and Nancy Neuenschwander, *Two Friends in Love: Growing Together in Marriage* (Portland, OR: Multnomah Press, 1986), p. 135.

Chapter 8: Roles, Responsibilities, and Decision-Making

1. Dwight H. Small, *Christian: Celebrate Your Sexuality* (Old Tappan, NJ: Revell, 1974), p. 144.
2. Dennis Guernsey, *Thoroughly Married* (Waco, TX: Word Books, 1976), p. 70.
3. James Olthuis, *I Pledge Thee My Troth* (New York: Harper & Row, 1975), p. 27.

Chapter 10: Communication

1. Reuel Howe, *Herein Is Love* (Valley Forge, PA: Judson Press, 1961), p. 100.
2. David and Vera Mace, *We Can Have Better Marriages If We Really Want Them* (Nashville: Abingdon Press, 1974).
3. Albert Metowbian, *Silent Messages* (Belmont, CA: Wadsworth Publishing Company, 1971), pp. 42-44.

4. Adapted from John Powell, *Why Am I Afraid to Tell You Who I Am?* (Niles, IL: Argus Communications, 1969), pp. 54-62.
5. Adapted from Ross Campbell, *How to Really Love Your Child* (Wheaton, IL: Victor Books, 1977), p. 20.
6. Paul Tournier, *To Understand Each Other* (Richmond, VA: John Knox Press, 1967), p. 29.

Chapter 11: Conflict (or "Sound the Battle Cry")

1. James G.T. Fairfield, *When You Don't Agree* (Scottdale, PA: Herald Press, 1977), pp. 33, 34, 231.

Chapter 12: Finances

1. Ron and Judy Blue, *Money Talks and So Can We,* (Grand Rapids, MI: Zondervan Publishers, 1999).

Chapter 14: Your Spiritual Life Together

1. Howard and Jeanne Hendricks, gen. eds. with La Vonne Neff, *Husbands and Wives* (Wheaton, IL: Victor Books, 1988), p. 158.
2. Adapted from Donald R. Harvey, *The Spiritually Intimate Marriage* (Grand Rapids, MI: Fleming H. Revell, 1991), p. 24.

A Closing Thought

1. Elizabeth Achtemeier, *The Committed Marriage* (Philadelphia: Westminster Press, 1976), p. 41.

Recommended Reading

H. Norman Wright, *Holding On to Romance* (Ventura, CA: Regal Books, 1992).

H. Norman Wright, *Secrets of a Lasting Marriage* (Ventura, CA: Regal Books, 1995).

H. Norman Wright and Gary J. Oliver. *How to Bring Out the Best in Your Spouse* (Ann Arbor, MI: Servant Publications, 1997).

Other Books
by H. Norman Wright

Before You Say "I Do"

Before You Remarry

Finding Your Perfect Mate

Quiet Moments for Couples

Quiet Times for Couples

Quiet Times for Couples Perpetual Calendar

Quiet Times for Parents

Training Christians to Counsel

Quiet Moments in the Garden

Quiet Times for Couples

by H. Norman Wright

Designed to stimulate genuinely open communication between you and your mate, *Quiet Times for Couples* provides a framework for conversation, making it easier for you to share the deeper parts of your lives.

Bestselling author H. Norman Wright shares wisdom gained from many years of counseling experience on subjects geared specifically to couples—wisdom that will draw you closer as you seek God together each day.

Quiet Times for Couples is an excellent gift book for special occasions—weddings, anniversaries, and rededications.

NOTES

NOTES

NOTES

NOTES

NOTES

NOTES

NOTES

NOTES

NOTES

NOTES